A Crescent Kept

NURTURING WITHOUT EXHAUSTING

AANCHAL KAKKAR

BLUEROSE PUBLISHERS
India | U.K.

Copyright © Aanchal Kakkar 2025

All rights reserved by author. No part of this publication may be reproduced, stored in a retrieval system or transmitted in any form or by any means, electronic, mechanical, photocopying, recording or otherwise, without the prior permission of the author. Although every precaution has been taken to verify the accuracy of the information contained herein, the publisher assume no responsibility for any errors or omissions. No liability is assumed for damages that may result from the use of information contained within.

BlueRose Publishers takes no responsibility for any damages, losses, or liabilities that may arise from the use or misuse of the information, products, or services provided in this publication.

For permissions requests or inquiries regarding this publication, please contact:

BLUEROSE PUBLISHERS
www.BlueRoseONE.com
info@bluerosepublishers.com
+91 8882 898 898
+4407342408967

ISBN: 978-93-7018-093-2

Cover design: Daksh
Typesetting: Tanya Raj Upadhyay

First Edition: May 2025

About the Book

Parenting is a journey of love, but does it have to be exhausting?

A Crescent Kept, helps you to discover the art of raising a child with warmth and care—without losing yourself as parents in the process. Inspired by the quiet resilience of the crescent moon, this book offers a heartfelt guide to nurture your little one while preserving your energy, identity, and peace of mind.

Through personal reflections, practical insights, and gentle wisdom, this book explores:

- Creating a deep, lasting bond with your child without feeling exhausted.
- Taking good care of yourself is taking good care of your child.
- Finding balance in the ever changing phases of parenting.
- Embracing imperfections and releasing the guilt of "not doing enough"

Parenting is not about shining at full brightness all the time—it's about being a steady, comforting presence, just like the moon. *A Crescent Kept* is your invitation to nurture with love, live with balance, and embrace the beauty of parenting without exhaustion. Between pages of normalizing self-paced parenting and the gamut of varied emotions, you will find heartfelt anecdotes, relatable challenges and a lot of parenting trivia.

Acknowledgement

The journey of this book started not when my pen hit the paper first time, but when the tiny seed started blossoming within me. The whirlwind of emotions acted as the foundation and my own immediate atmosphere formed it's orbit.

I owe this book, in part, to both my children—

One, whose heartbeat I could not hold on to, yet who lives on in the quiet corners of my soul.

And the other, whose laughter and presence continue to save me every single day.

One taught me the weight of love that never got to bloom,

The other reminds me of the light that still grows in its place.

This book is for them—

For the child I carry in memory,

And the child who carries me forward.

Hope you enjoy reading this manifesto of light-hearted parenting as much I loved writing it.

-**Aanchal Kakkar**

About the Author

Aanchal Kakkar is a writer, mother, and lifelong learner. Formerly a publishing professional in the field of computer science, she now uses her voice to support fellow parents through the highs and lows of raising children. *The Crescent Kept* is her heartfelt debut, inspired by real conversations and quiet realizations.

While embracing motherhood, Aanchal felt a deep void—one that many parents silently experience.

Determined to understand how others navigate the delicate balance between professional life and parenting, Aanchal began heartfelt conversations with parents across the country. These discussions, documented in a personal journal, became the foundation for *A Crescent Kept: Nurturing Without Exhausting*—a book dedicated to helping parents nurture their children without losing themselves in the process.

Beyond writing, Aanchal is passionate about recommending meaningful stories, books, and sustainable toys that inspire both parents and children. Through these efforts, Aanchal hopes to encourage parents to embrace their own identity while raising the next generation with love, wisdom, and balance.

SAMVYAN_E_VERSE

Moon made me happy, but I miss pie

The light of the moon shines so bright
Seems like a friend in the quiet.
The gentle warmth from the cold wind
Just like we are whispering our dreams.
I am happy, I am fine
Yet deep inside, something is bothering me
Which I cannot hide.
Holding my child in my arms
Was the piece of joy I ever wanted.
The moon is shining so high
But I still miss my Pie…
I am still looking for my heavenly father,
Gazing up in the sky.
I look at the moon but miss my Pie!
Is he watching me beyond the stars?
Can he hear the words I am whispering to him?
I often tell my daughter the stories he once used to tell me
But I am missing his voice just one more time.
The moon is glowing, the wind is blowing
Yet its warmth can never take his place.
The world is moving on, and so everyone is, including me
But in my heart, I still miss my Pie.

{A poem dedicated to my father, who was a piece of happiness (Pie) in my life.}

Somewhere between the quiet of the night and my daughter's soft sighs, I find myself missing my father's guidance and support. Every time I look at the moon, I wonder if he's watching us from wherever he is. *If he knows how much I wish I could call him, hear his laughter, and share even the smallest details of my day. If he knows that I tell my daughter about him—about his love for the moon and how he had a way of making ordinary moments feel magical.*

Raising a child is a beautiful journey, but some nights, the weight of love and loss lingers beside me like an old friend.

Table of Contents

Introduction 1

Chapter 1: Normalize Missing Who We Were 4

Chapter 2: Invest In Yourself 9

Chapter 3: Creating Balance 16

Chapter 4: Creating A New "You" 22

Chapter 5: Embracing The Unknown 28

Chapter 6: Parenthood and Relationships:
Navigating Growth, Love, and Change 34

Chapter 7: The Silent Battles Parents Fight 41

Chapter 8: Holding On to Letting Go 46

Chapter 9: Children Teach Us 54

Chapter 10: Finding Myself in the Moonlight 58

Introduction

A Crescent Kept: Nurturing Without Exhausting is a heartfelt exploration of parenthood, balance, and the deep emotional journey of raising a child while staying true to oneself. This book delves into the art of nurturing with love and patience—without losing energy or personal identity in the process. Through personal reflections, insightful strategies, and gentle reminders, *A Crescent Kept* offers guidance for parents who want to cultivate a meaningful bond with their children without feeling overwhelmed or exhausted.

This book draws inspiration from the crescent moon—a symbol of quiet strength, resilience, and the beauty of growth in phases. Just as the moon never disappears but simply changes its form, this book reassures parents that even in moments of exhaustion, their presence and love remain powerful and constant.

If you're a new parent navigating sleepless nights and want to seek a renewed sense of balance, *A Crescent Kept* is an invitation to embrace parenthood with grace, mindfulness, and an open heart.

My first witness to parenthood is -The moon. Just like the moon's softness, calmness, and presence in the night sky creates a sense of peace and tranquillity, helping to soothe anxieties and promote relaxation.

Similarly, a parent's presence or even the absence continues to comfort, calm, guide, and watch over their children. The moonlight reassures us that no matter parents' love towards their children, it will last forever. Parenthood is a whirlwind—endless tasks, scattered toys, and a to-do list that never seems to shrink. It's an unpredictable journey, messy and overwhelming at times. There are moments when exhaustion takes over, patience wears thin, and nothing goes as planned. Some days feel tangled, as our children test our limits, reminding us that love is not always neat or easy.

A silent battle wages within us—to give everything to our children while secretly longing to reconnect with the person we used to be. Parenthood collides with the memories of "before." But it's not just about the chaos, the exhaustion, or the sacrifices. It's also about the stillness of the night, when the world sleeps, but our minds race with thoughts that refuse to rest.

Did I do enough today?
Did I hold them close enough?
Am I a good parent?
Will my child trust me with their worries?
Will they think of me as their safe place?
Are they growing the way they should?
What more can I do for them?
Have I secured their future?
How can I help them thrive?

These questions haunt every parent. Our minds and bodies may grow weary, but our hearts never stop worrying. Each night, the moon keeps us company. Our children may not remember our sleepless nights, but we will always be there for them, because we are ***parents.***

The strangest thing about parenthood is how it sneaks up on you. One day, you're someone's child; the next, you're the one answering small voices in the night, the one whose embrace is the safest place in the world.

And yet, even as we cradle our children, we long for the warmth we once knew—the scent of our father's arms, the taste of our mother's cooking, the comfort of slow mornings, the luxury of *"me time"*.

Time moves forward, unstoppable. One day, our children will outgrow our arms. Their small hands will slip from ours as they reach for the world. The moon will still shine, watching over them, just as it once watched over us.

Maybe, years from now, they will stand on their own, searching for something familiar—the warmth of home, the love we poured into them. Maybe then, they will miss us, just as we miss our parents. They will remember how we nurtured them without pause, how their needs became our priority, how we gave of ourselves without hesitation.

As parents, we hope to pass the same light to our children that once illuminated our own paths. Every day, we long for someone to confide in, someone who understands without judgment.

But parenthood is not just about the first steps, the first words, the first giggles. It's about the quiet moments—the ones that may seem ordinary now but will one day become the most cherished memories of all.

Chapter 1:
Normalize Missing Who We Were

At night, when the world sleeps, a parent's mind remains awake, whispering memories of our childhood. We recall the way our parents' voices soothed us when we spoke of dreams, life, and things we were too young to understand but old enough to feel. We once felt safe, wrapped in the warmth of their love. The same moon shines upon us now, but the night feels different—because today, we are the safe place for our children.

The moon—like our children—fills us with joy, yet we still miss our older selves. Once, we lived without the weight of responsibility, free of endless worries, moving through life with ease. Sometimes, we long to experience that again.

The moon is both comfort and longing, watching over us as we raise our children, reliving the moments we once shared with our parents. Even if they are no longer with us, the moon bridges the past and present, linking the love we received to the love we now give.

Time moves forward, unstoppable. One day, our children will outgrow our arms, their small hands slipping from ours as they step into the world. Yet the moon will still shine on them, just as it shines on us.

The transition from carefree sleeping to conscious resting is profound. Doubts creep in—self-judgment, guilt, the realization that we have changed. This shift in identity—from woman to mother, from man to father—can be overwhelming. At times, it may even leave us feeling lost.

But when we see our children looking to us with wonder, we understand that love is about giving—not because we must, but because we *want* to.

And maybe, deep down, we all know this truth. Missing our past selves after becoming parents is universal, yet rarely spoken about.

The sacrifices of parenthood are not easily recognized, but missing who we once were does not mean we are lost.

- Just as the moon moves through phases, so does parenthood. Some days, we feel on top of the world. Other days, we are exhausted, frustrated, and emotionally drained. This ebb and flow is natural, reminding us that nothing is permanent.

- Becoming a parent doesn't mean loving every part of the transition. Missing our old selves does not mean we love our children any less. It simply means we are evolving, and with growth comes some loss.

- We should never regret this journey. The person we were didn't vanish—we simply stretched, made room for something profound. It's okay to grieve the quiet moments that once belonged to us. It's okay to miss the ease of rest without guilt.

- Parenthood does not erase who we were—it adds layers of experience. We may miss our past selves, but we can honour them in small ways, practicing self-care and embracing both the love and the loss in our hearts.

- The ache of missing our old selves lingers in the background of our days—in the late-night rocking, the messy rooms, the car rides where we were once independent and carefree. But this ache reminds us that growth always requires trade-offs.

- Our past selves still live within us, just in a new way. The late-night adventures have shifted to lullabies; the spontaneous drives have turned into family nights. It's okay to miss who we were—and it's also okay to become someone just as worthy. We are shaped by love that stretches beyond ourselves.

- As parents, we should honour who we were while embracing who we are becoming.

We are not lost in parenthood—we are expanding with it. It is perfectly okay to miss the past while loving the present.

Kiran's journey: Normalizing Missing Your Older Self in Parenthood

Kiran, a 30-year-old former blogger from Delhi and an avid traveler, had always thrived on spontaneity. Her days were filled with last-minute trips, impromptu live sessions, and coffee-fueled meetings. But when she became a mother to her daughter, Peanut, she embraced parenthood wholeheartedly. Yet, deep down, she couldn't shake the feeling of missing the vibrant identity she once had.

Challenges Faced

Her last-minute adventures were replaced with the strict nap schedules. She was finding herself who she used to be and what she has become. Missing her old self made her guilty of not accepting parenthood completely.

Embracing the Feeling

Instead of suppressing her emotions, Kiran normalizes missing her older self while she still embraces her motherhood journey. She started writing what she used to do and motivated others with her writings. She started giving coaching to influencers on how to become a famous blogger.

She integrated her pre-mom self to current-mom self and bought adventures into parenting by storytelling and travelling with her daughter.

Outcome

Kiran did not choose between her past self and her current self. She accepted the longing, which didn't diminish her love for her child, and she wholeheartedly accepted that longing for her old life was natural. She had new experiences with her daughter, she made good memories with her daughter, which made their bond stronger.

Chapter 2:
Invest In Yourself

What did you do before becoming a parent? Are you still doing it? Does parenting take up all your time, leaving you longing for your older self?

Here are some ways to nurture yourself while navigating parenthood:

- ***Taking time for yourself is not selfish.*** Parenthood asks us to give so much of ourselves, but we cannot pour from an empty cup. Prioritizing our well-being allows us to show up as better parents.

- ***Your health matters most.*** Sleep when exhaustion takes over, nourish your body with nutritious food, and remember that taking care of yourself is essential, not optional.

- ***Keep learning and growing.*** Read, take online classes, or explore new hobbies. Even dedicating 20–25 minutes to something you love can reconnect you with the person you were before parenthood.

- ***Be present with your child.*** Engage in their world—play their favorite games, explore their interests, and create alongside them. Bonding over creativity, storytelling, or baking builds memories that will last a lifetime.

- ***Build a support system.*** Parenthood is not meant to be a solo journey. Lean on true friends, family, or parenting communities. Accepting help is not a sign of weakness; it's a way to recharge.

- ***Set small, attainable goals.*** Whether it's fitness, career growth, or creative projects, having personal goals keeps you motivated and reminds you that your dreams still matter.

- ***Make time for solitude.*** Whether it's exercise, yoga, journaling, a walk, or simply enjoying a warm cup of tea, find moments to reconnect with yourself. "Me time" is not a luxury—it's a necessity.

- ***Explore work-from-home opportunities.*** If stepping outside for work isn't an option, look for flexible income streams.

- ***Embrace change with a positive mindset.*** Start your day with gratitude, reflect on your journey, and welcome new opportunities. Confidence comes from acknowledging growth and adaptation.

- ***Honor your past self while embracing the present.*** It's okay to miss the person you used to be. Parenthood doesn't erase who we were—it simply adds new layers of experience and growth. Cherish the memories of your past while creating new ones with your children.

- ***Recognize that transformation is natural.*** Like the moon moving through phases, we, too, evolve as parents. Some days feel overwhelming, while others shine with joy. Embrace the ebb and flow of this journey.

- ***Finding joy in small moments.*** A child's laughter, the warmth of their embrace, or a whispered "I love you" in the dark—these are the twinkling moments that make the tangled day's worth it.

Phases of parenthood will change, but they should not erase your identity. Investing in yourself is the best gift you can give—to yourself and to your child, who will learn the importance of self-love and balance by watching you.

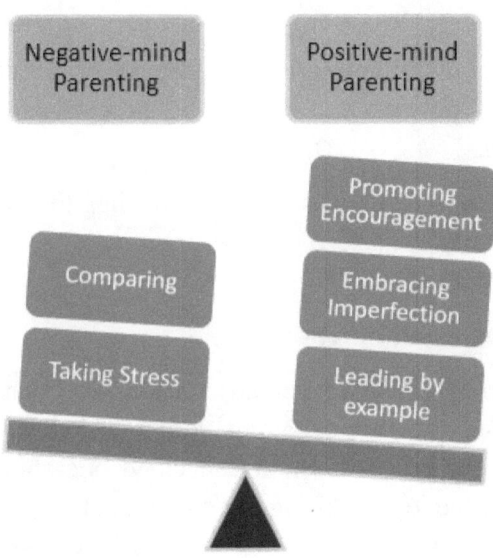

Positive-mind parenting VS Negative-mind parenting

Positive Mind Parenting is about approaching parenthood with optimism, mindfulness, and emotional resilience. It focuses on nurturing children with love, patience, and understanding while also maintaining a positive mindset as a parent.

Key Principles of Positive Mind Parenting:

Mindful Presence – Being fully present with your child, cherishing small moments, and responding with patience instead of reacting with frustrations.

Encouragement Over Criticism – Using words that uplift and motivate rather than discourage.

Leading by Example – Children always learn by observing their parents.So, try to teach them kindness and gratitude with your actions.

Embracing Imperfection – Instead of focusing on a "perfect" parent,try to become a "present" parent to your children.

Self-Care is Not Selfish – Understanding that a happy and emotionally balanced parent raises a confident and emotionally secure child.

Negative-Mind Parenting

Sometimes a negative mindset takes over when we are exhausted in the parenting journey. Self-doubt, guilt, frustration, and exhaustion can cloud our ability to fully embrace the joy of raising our children. Here's how to shift from negativity to positivity, as a positive mind is always better than a negative mind:

- Recognize when you are overwhelmed and ask for help.
- Avoid comparison—every child and parent has a unique journey.
- Instead of dwelling on daily struggles, focus on small wins.

- Reframe mistakes as learning opportunities for both you and your child.
- Take rest and allow yourself grace on tough days.
- Seek support and surround yourself with uplifting influences.

Parenthood is tangled, chaotic, and sometimes exhausting, but within the whirlwind, there are twinkling moments—ones that remind us that even as we evolve, we are still *us*.

Kabir's Journey: Investing in Yourself

Background

Kabir, a 37-year-old guitarist and cricketer from Mumbai, thrived in his career and had a deep passion for marathons, games, and cricket. His life was dynamic, filled with personal achievements and social connections. But when he and his wife welcomed their son, everything shifted. While he embraced fatherhood wholeheartedly, he unknowingly started neglecting himself. His cricket bat gathered dust, his running shoes remained untouched for months, and his social circle felt like a distant memory.

Challenges Faced

Balancing work, personal passions, and parenting felt like an impossible equation. Every moment spent on himself felt like stolen time—time that should belong to his son. He struggled with the transition, feeling torn between his new identity as a father and the person he used to be. The guilt of missing his old self weighed heavily on him.

The Shift

Kabir realized that to be the best father he could be, he needed to nurture himself too. He made small yet intentional changes:

- He reintroduced self-care into his routine—waking up early to exercise and play his guitar a few days in a week.

- He and his wife created a system where both had dedicated "me time" each week, free from guilt.

- He reconnected with friends, slowly reviving his social life.

- Instead of feeling guilty for personal time, he reframed it as an investment in his well-being—an investment that made him a more patient, present, and an engaged father.

Outcome

As Kabir started reinvesting in himself, he felt a renewed sense of energy and joy. He realized that prioritizing himself didn't take away from his parenting—it enhanced it. He became more patient, more engaged, and more content. The guilt faded, replaced by the understanding that balance wasn't just possible—it was essential.

This journey helped him redefine parenthood, proving that being a great parent doesn't mean losing yourself but evolving into a fuller, happier version of who you were before.

Chapter 3: Creating Balance

We've often heard from previous generations:

"We raised five or six kids, and you're struggling with just one or two?"

But no matter how "well" we turned out, the choices made by past generations shouldn't define how we parent today. Science, technology, and societal expectations have evolved, and parenting is no longer a one-size-fits-all journey. It's unpredictable—filled with highs and lows, triumphs and struggles.

Every child is unique, and so is every parenting experience. Embracing the *non-linear* nature of parenthood is crucial because growth happens in waves, not straight lines. Finding balance isn't about perfection—it's an ongoing process.

Some days, everything will feel off, and that's okay. It's time to normalize the fact that parenting doesn't have to look effortless.

Here's how to create balance while navigating the chaos of parenthood:

- ***Balance benefits both you and your child.*** When you prioritize a balanced approach, you nurture your child while also taking care of yourself. A well-supported parent is more present, patient, and emotionally available.

- ***Establish routines but allow flexibility.*** Set a structure for both yourself and your child, but don't be rigid. Let them explore within safe boundaries. There should be a balance between guiding them and allowing hands-on learning.

- ***Discipline should be about teaching, not punishing.*** Setting clear goals is important, but expecting a child to meet them without acknowledging their emotions can be damaging. Teach accountability with kindness, showing them that learning from mistakes is part of growth. Be a companion in their journey rather than just a guide.

- ***Don't lose yourself in the parenting process.*** Your mental well-being is just as important as your child's. A joyful, rested parent is far better than an exhausted, frustrated one. Parenting is a huge part of your identity, but it's not the only part. You are still an individual with dreams, passions, and personal needs.

- ***Teach independence and responsibility.*** Your child needs unconditional love, but they also need structure. Allow them to express their emotions freely while learning to take responsibility. Teach them that household responsibilities should be gender-neutral—everyone contributes, regardless of gender.

- ***Protect, but don't shelter***. While keeping your child safe is a priority, allowing them space to grow is just as essential. Give them the freedom to make mistakes, experience challenges, and learn resilience. Encourage exploration and persistence, even when they struggle. Let them fall, but teach them to get back up.

- ***Encourage problem-solving rather than fixing everything***. Listen when they come to you with their concerns, but instead of rushing to solve their problems, guide them in finding solutions. This builds confidence and critical thinking.

- ***Prioritize quality time over quantity.*** Avoid distractions when you're with your child. A few minutes of true connection—fully engaged, with no phones or work stress—means more than hours of distracted presence.

- ***Be open to learning from your child***. Parenting isn't just about teaching—it's also about listening. Children have unique perspectives and can teach us new ways of seeing the world. Stay open to their wisdom.

- *Admit when you're wrong.* Acknowledging mistakes teaches children that it's okay to be imperfect. They'll learn accountability by watching how you handle your missteps.

- *Find joy in small moments.* Parenting isn't just about milestones—it's about the ordinary, everyday magic. Laugh together, celebrate the little victories, and be present in the now. Future plans matter, but so does enjoying the moment.

- ***Parenting is messy, imperfect, and sometimes exhausting.*** Some days, you will feel balanced; other days, you won't—and that's okay. Let go of the guilt.

- ***Creating balance doesn't mean having it all figured out***—it means adjusting, adapting, and allowing space for both structure and spontaneity. Parenthood isn't about doing everything perfectly; it's about being present, being human, and loving deeply.

At the end of the day, what truly matters is the bond you share with your child. You are both learning, growing, and adjusting together in this beautiful, tangled journey of parenthood.

Shweta's Journey: Balancing Parenthood and Career

Shweta, a 39-year-old single mother from Gurugram working in an IT company, has faced constant struggles in balancing her parental responsibilities with her professional duties. The pressures of work often left her feeling overwhelmed, missing out on precious moments with her daughter, and stuck in a monotonous routine. She longed to create special memories with her daughter, but as a single mother, finding time for both herself and her child seemed impossible.

Challenges:

- Managing household and work responsibilities alone while ensuring quality time with her daughter.
- Feeling exhausted and emotionally drained from juggling multiple roles.
- Experiencing guilt over not being present enough for her daughter.
- Struggling with a lack of personal time and self-care.

Strategies Implemented:

- *Time Management:* Shweta began prioritizing tasks, distinguishing between urgent and important parenting and work-related activities.
- *Setting Boundaries*: She established clear boundaries at work and created dedicated family time, ensuring she was fully present for her daughter.

- ***Shared Responsibilities:*** She hired a professional caretaker to assist with household chores and childcare, allowing her to rest and recharge.
- ***Self-Care and Mindfulness*****:** To strengthen their bond, Shweta and her daughter joined hobby classes together.
- ***Seeking Support*****:** She connected with a parenting group and had open discussions with her employer about flexible work arrangements, including remote work options.

Results:

- A stronger emotional connection with her daughter.
- Reduced parental stress and improved mental well-being.
- Better ability to manage work demands without compromising quality time with her child.
- Increased satisfaction in both parenting and professional life.

Conclusion:

By setting boundaries, prioritizing family time, and sharing responsibilities, Shweta successfully created a healthier balance between parenthood and work. Her story highlights the importance of intentional parenting, effective time management, and self-care in fostering a fulfilling family life while maintaining career growth.

Chapter 4: Creating A New "You"

I was a free bird before you arrived,

I thought I knew the shape of mine.

But when you came, so small,

You reshaped my world entirely.

My hands once built dreams just for myself,

Now, they gently hold you close.

My carefree sleep has turned into soft lullabies,

Whispering love in every note.

My past has been traded for moments with you,

And with each passing day, my love grows anew.

I always knew you were a part of me,

But in you, I have found myself again.

Yes, you are a parent—but that's not all you are. You are still *you*—a dreamer, a thinker, a person with passions, interests, and goals. It's okay to nurture your own identity while nurturing your child.

But let's be honest—parenthood can feel overwhelming. The joy is immense, but so are the emotional shifts that can leave you feeling lost.

You may wonder: *How do I carve out space for myself in this chaos?*

- Yes, your ***life is changing***. Your responsibilities are growing. Your heart is overflowing with love, but at times, it feels stretched thin. Beneath the diapers, sleepless nights, endless worries, and constant giving, *you* still matter. You are worthy of joy, of rest, of dreams.

- ***Don't lose yourself in the journey***. Remember, the same moon you once gazed at as a child is the same moon your child admires now. Your old self isn't lost—it just needs to be rediscovered. Find small ways to bring back the things that once made you feel alive. Even if it's just for 10-15 minutes a day, it can transform your spirit.

- ***You don't have to do everything alone***. Asking for help isn't a sign of weakness—it's a recognition of your own worth. Whether it's an hour of rest, a quiet walk, or simply breathing without interruption, you *deserve* that time.

- ***Parenthood isn't a solo journey***, nor should it be bound by gender roles. Raising a child is a shared responsibility. Support should flow both ways, because when parents lift each other up, they build a stronger, happier home.

Embrace yourself. Your identity doesn't vanish with parenthood—it evolves. And in that evolution, you will find a new, stronger, and even more beautiful version of *you*.

In parenthood, there are moments when everything feels perfectly aligned—the first time your baby smiles at you, the way their tiny fingers curl around yours, or the quiet realization of just how deeply you've connected with your child.

But just as the moon moves through its cycles, we too evolve as parents. And with that evolution comes the bittersweet feeling of leaving behind parts of our old selves. It's natural to grieve those changes, to wonder if we are losing who we once were.

Yet, just as the moon never truly disappears, neither do we. This journey is not about losing ourselves—it's about transforming. It's about understanding that with every phase of change, we gain something new, something just as beautiful, just as fulfilling.

Sumit's Journey: Rediscovering Himself in Parenthood

Before fatherhood, Sumit from Nagpur was a dreamer, and a businessman. He had goals, passions, and a clear sense of who he was. But when his son arrived, everything shifted. The world that once revolved around his dreams now centered on this tiny human.

At first, he embraced it wholeheartedly, pouring every ounce of love and energy into his son. But over time, something inside him felt... lost. The person he once was seemed like a distant memory. His days blurred into a cycle of office to home, home to office, interrupted sleep, and the beautiful chaos of raising a child. Yet, deep inside, a quiet voice whispered: *Where am I in all of this?*

Then, one evening, as he watched his son gaze at the stars with wide, curious eyes, something clicked. The same stars Sumit had admired as a child, the same one that had once fueled his dreams, was now lighting up his son's wonder. In that moment, he realized—he wasn't lost. He was simply evolving.

Rediscovering Himself in Parenthood

Determined to find balance, Sumit made small but meaningful changes:

- **Reclaiming His Passions:** Instead of giving up his passion for astronomy, he shared it with his son—teaching him to use telescopes or simply lying beside him, gazing up at the stars.
- **Prioritizing Self-Care:** Even if it was just 10 minutes of journaling or a quiet cup of tea, he carved out moments that were his alone.

- **Letting Go of Guilt:** He embraced the truth that being a good parent didn't mean sacrificing his identity—it meant showing his child what it meant to be whole.

As time passed, Sumit no longer felt he had lost himself. Instead, he had found a new version of himself—one that was stronger, wiser, and deeply enriched by the journey of fatherhood.

Parenthood isn't about choosing between your child and yourself. It's about growing together, evolving, and embracing the *new you* that emerges along the way.

Chapter 5:
Embracing The Unknown

Is it our duty to figure everything out on our own?

No, Just like a new moon, there is a quiet beauty in the unknown.

Parenthood isn't about having all the answers—it's about navigating the *tangled days* and finding peace in the *twinkling nights*, embracing each moment as it comes.

- *Find joy in flexibility.* Some days will be chaotic, filled with endless to-do lists, unexpected messes, and exhaustion. Other nights will be magical, with sleepy cuddles, whispered lullabies, and the soft glow of your child's wonder. Adjust to the rhythm—sometimes, *going with the flow* is the best way to move forward.

- *You are never alone in this journey.* Every parent struggles in their way. Just as the stars shine brighter together, lean on those who understand—seek support, share stories, and know that no one has to do this alone.

- *Parenting is never perfect.* No matter how much you give, something will always be left undone. But just as the moon is never truly gone, neither are the moments you miss. What matters is the love that fills the spaces in between.

- *Plan for the future, but embrace the present.* The days may feel tangled with responsibilities, but the nights remind us to pause. Watch your child's eyes light up at something simple. Hold their tiny hand a little longer. These are the moments that become the brightest stars in your memories.

- *Let go of judgment.* People will always have opinions, but your peace matters more than their words. *You* know your child best. Trust in your love, your instincts, and the path you are creating together.

- *Hard days don't last forever.* Just as twinkling stars emerge after the darkest nights, joy follows struggle. Even when parenthood feels overwhelming, remember: the chaos of today is shaping the love and strength of tomorrow.

- *Parenthood is full of surprises.* No matter how much we prepare, some moments will leave us unsure of what to do. And that's okay. Some of the most beautiful lessons are found in the unknown.

- *The journey is yours alone.* The days may be tangled with challenges, but every twinkling night is a reminder of how far you've come. No two parenting paths are the same, so trust in yours.

Parenthood is a journey of waxing and waning moments—a delicate balance of chaos and calm, exhaustion and wonder. But within it all lies love, growth, and deep connections. Like a crescent moon, you don't have to shine at full brightness to be enough.

Trust yourself !!

Stay present !!

Let each phase unfold with grace, knowing that even in the dimmest light, you are still a guiding force. Take a deep breath, lean into the journey, and know that you are exactly where you need to be.

Sunita and Sameer's journey: Embracing the Unknown
Background

Sunita and Sameer from Noida were preparing to become first-time parents with excitement and meticulous planning. They attended prenatal classes, devoured parenting books, and lovingly set up the perfect nursery, believing they had everything figured out. But parenthood, like the night sky, is unpredictable—sometimes tangled with challenges, twinkling with unexpected beauty.

Their journey took an unforeseen turn when their baby was born prematurely at just 30 weeks, requiring an extended stay in the NICU.

The Struggles They Never Anticipated

- Their newborn struggled with breathing difficulties and feeding challenges, filling their days with worry, exhaustion, and endless hospital visits.
- Instead of bringing their baby home to a beautifully decorated nursery, they found themselves navigating the sterile, beeping environment of the NICU, counting the minutes between updates from doctors.
- Fear crept in as they questioned whether they were strong enough for this unexpected path.

Finding Beauty in the Unexpected

- They realized that parenting was never about perfect plans—it was about resilience, adaptability, and love.
- Instead of dwelling on what they couldn't control, they focused on what they *could*—supporting each other and being present for their child.

- They became students of this new reality, learning from doctors and nurses, absorbing every bit of knowledge that would help their baby thrive.

- They celebrated small victories—the first time their baby latched onto a bottle, the first time the oxygen monitor showed improvement—recognizing that even the tiniest progress was a step forward.

- They let go of their expectations and embraced each moment, knowing that even amidst uncertainty, their love was the one constant their baby could always rely on.

Outcome: Love Stronger Than Fear

- Their child grew stronger day by day, nurtured not only by medical care but by the unwavering love of their parents. Eventually, after weeks of tangled days, they finally brought their baby home—a moment that felt even more magical than they had ever imagined.

- Their plans may not have unfolded as expected, but their journey led them to something even more profound—a deep, unshakable bond with their child and with each other.

- They learned that parenthood will always bring surprises, but within those surprises lies immense joy. Each challenge is an opportunity to grow, to love more deeply, and to trust the journey.

- Parenthood isn't about having all the answers—it's about embracing each phase, finding glow in the dim moments, and trusting that even the most uncertain days will lead to a gentle, guiding light, just like a crescent kept in the night sky.

Most importantly, **BELIEVE IN YOURSELF!**

Chapter 6:
Parenthood and Relationships: Navigating Growth, Love, and Change

Parenting is often described as a transformative journey—one that reshapes not only our identities but also our relationships. As parents, the dynamics with a spouse, partner, family, and friends inevitably shift. This change brings both beauty and challenges. While the tangled days may be filled with stress, exhaustion, and misunderstandings, the twinkling nights serve as a reminder of deep love, shared dreams, and the new connections forged along the way.

The Evolving Relationship between Partners

Parenting is a journey that takes two individuals from being a couple to becoming a family, then to becoming parents. With each stage, their roles shift, and they grow into a team responsible for nurturing a child. This transition is filled with both joys and struggles.

From "Us" to "Three (or More)"

- As partners, they are no longer just a couple but a team working to meet their child's needs.
- Romantic moments are now intertwined with sleepless nights, duties, and responsibilities.
- Spontaneous getaways are replaced with carefully planned family trips.

- Stress and exhaustion can sometimes turn minor misunderstandings into major conflicts.
- Instead of blaming each other, partners who learn to express their feelings, appreciate one another, and work as a team can strengthen their bond, not just with each other but also with their children.

Keeping the Connection Alive

- Small gestures—like holding hands, weekly coffee dates, or simply checking in on each other—can help maintain an emotional connection.
- Partners should intentionally carve out **10-15 minutes daily** to reconnect, even amidst parenting chaos.
- It's essential to remember that before becoming parents, they were partners first. Nurturing their relationship strengthens the foundation of their family.
- Both parents must acknowledge that they are adapting to new roles and should **support rather than criticize** one another.

Parenting is not just about raising a child—it's about **growing together as a couple while embracing the new phase of life with love, patience, and teamwork.**

Parenting Impacts Friendship Bonds

Friendships naturally evolve, shaped by shifting priorities, responsibilities, and lifestyles. One of the most significant transitions occurs when someone becomes a parent.

As life takes on new meaning, social circles may shift. Parents often find themselves connecting more with others who understand the joys and struggles of raising a child. Late-night hangouts and spontaneous meetups may no longer be possible, and friends without children might not fully grasp the exhaustion, responsibilities, or the constant demands of parenting. This can sometimes create distance, not out of a lack of love but due to the simple reality of different life paths.

However, **true friendships withstand change**. While some friends may drift apart, others will adapt, offering patience, understanding, and support. It's important to stay connected with those who uplift and encourage you, regardless of their parental status. Surrounding yourself with people who acknowledge the ups and downs of parenting can provide valuable guidance and a much-needed emotional anchor.

Finding New Friendships and Support

Parenthood also opens doors to new connections. Engaging in **parenting groups, support networks, and online communities** can introduce you to people who share similar experiences. These friendships can offer practical advice, emotional reassurance, and the comfort of knowing you're not alone in this journey.

Some ways to build meaningful connections as a parent include:

- **Joining local parent groups or playdate meetups** to bond with like-minded individuals.
- **Participating in online forums or parenting communities** where you can share insights and seek guidance.

- **Attending family-friendly events or workshops** to meet parents who understand your journey.
- **Maintaining intentional efforts with old friends**—even a quick call or message can keep the bond alive.

While parenting may change the nature of friendships, it also deepens relationships in unexpected ways. Some friendships will grow stronger, others may fade, and new ones will emerge. What truly matters is surrounding yourself with people who respect your journey, support your growth, and remind you that friendship, much like parenthood, is about love, patience, and understanding.

The Relationship Between *You* and *You*

Becoming a parent often means losing a part of your identity. The transition from simply being *you* to being "Mom" or "Dad" can feel overwhelming. But amidst the beautiful chaos of parenthood, it's important to remember that taking care of yourself is also a vital part of being a good parent.

Make time for your personal growth—whether it's reading, exercising, or just sitting with your own thoughts. Parenthood doesn't mean giving up on the things you once loved. Instead, find creative ways to include your child in your interests. This not only strengthens your bond with them but also helps you reconnect with yourself.

Keeping the Spark Alive

- Parenthood often replaces romance with sleepless nights and endless responsibilities, but maintaining an emotional connection is essential.

- Express your feelings, have meaningful conversations, and take time for small gestures like coffee dates or simply appreciating each other's efforts. These little things make a big difference.
- Physical and emotional intimacy may change, but it shouldn't fade away. Nurturing your connection is just as important as raising your child.

Rather than just *surviving* parenthood, embrace it—together. Through communication, patience, and intentional love, relationships can not only endure but thrive. The challenging days create deeper understanding and stronger bonds, while the quiet nights, filled with whispered "I love yous," remind us why this journey is worth every moment.

Rohan and Sheetal's Parenthood Journey: Navigating Love and Challenges

The Beginning

Rohan and Sheetal from Assam welcomed their first child, Sam, two years after their marriage. Before becoming parents, they had spent seven years together, sharing common interests, enjoying quality time, and building a strong, loving relationship. However, the arrival of their baby brought unexpected challenges that tested their bond.

The Challenges

- **Loss of Individual Identity:** Sheetal, who was once a social and outgoing person, found herself completely immersed in motherhood. She felt like she had lost a part of herself. Rohan, too, struggled to juggle work pressures while embracing his role as a father.

- **Lack of Quality Time:** Late-night feedings and constant responsibilities left little time for meaningful conversations. Their interactions became focused solely on childcare duties.

- **Emotional Disconnect:** Despite loving each other, they felt distant and misunderstood. The lack of communication and intimacy led to frequent arguments over minor issues.

The Steps They Took

- *Prioritizing Self-Care:* They each set aside 30 minutes a day for themselves, whether for reading, exercising, or simply unwinding.

- *Reigniting Romance:* They planned weekly date nights, even if it was just 1-2 hours, to rekindle their connection. Small gestures helped them rebuild their emotional bond.

- **Open Communication:** They made it a habit to discuss their feelings and challenges, expressing gratitude for each other's efforts daily.
- **Sharing Responsibilities:** They divided parenting duties more fairly to reduce stress and ensure that neither felt overwhelmed.
- **Maintaining Intimacy:** While physical closeness had changed, they found new ways to stay connected—leaving notes for each other, appreciating small efforts, sharing hugs, and watching their favorite movies together on weekends.

The Outcome

Through conscious effort and mutual understanding, Rohan and Sheetal found their rhythm as parents while keeping their relationship strong. They learned that:

- Parenthood brings challenges, but open communication and teamwork strengthen the bond.
- Taking time for oneself enhances the ability to nurture relationships.
- Small gestures like kind words, hugs, and appreciation can reignite love.

With effort, understanding, and love, parenthood doesn't have to be a struggle. A couple's ability to adapt, grow, and support each other determines whether they emerge from this phase as two exhausted individuals or as a stronger, deeply connected team

Chapter 7:
The Silent Battles Parents Fight

Parenthood is a beautiful journey filled with laughter, love, and precious moments. Yet, behind the smiles and bedtime stories, many parents fight silent battles—struggles that are rarely spoken about but deeply felt.

For many, especially mothers, balancing their own identity while nurturing their child feels like an ongoing challenge. The desire to give their best to their child often comes at the cost of personal time, passions, and self-care.

Regardless of circumstances, parents experience a constant **battle with guilt**—the feeling of never doing enough. This guilt can be overwhelming, especially when societal pressures and unsolicited advice make them question their parenting choices.

Exhaustion becomes a daily reality. Sleepless nights, endless responsibilities, and the never-ending demands of raising a child can leave parents physically and emotionally drained.

Meanwhile, the relationship between partners often takes a backseat. Conversations that once revolved around dreams and shared interests are now centered around diaper changes, school runs, and responsibilities. The emotional and physical intimacy that once thrived can begin to fade.

As children grow, parents face the **heart-wrenching battle of letting go.** From their first day of school to the moment they move out for college, every milestone is bittersweet—a mix of pride and the aching realization that their little one is becoming independent.

The Unique Battle of Single Parents

For single parents, these struggles can feel twice as intense. Without a partner to share the emotional and physical load, they juggle multiple roles, often feeling overwhelmed and alone.

- *Emotional and Physical Exhaustion* – Carrying the full weight of decision-making, financial responsibilities, and caregiving can be isolating and draining.

- *Lack of Personal Time* – With no one to share the workload, finding even a few moments for self-care can feel like a luxury.

- *Social Judgment* – Single parents often face unfair criticism or assumptions about their ability to provide a "complete" upbringing.

- *Financial Pressure* – Managing expenses on a single income while ensuring the best for their child adds another layer of stress.

How Single Parents Can Overcome These Challenges:

- Leaning on friends, family, or support groups can provide much-needed encouragement and help lighten the load.

- Reminding themselves that they are doing their best and that perfection is never the goal.

- Seeking therapy or counseling when needed can offer a safe space to navigate stress and emotions.

- Small, meaningful interactions help strengthen the bond and bring joy to the journey.
- Parenthood is a journey of love, sacrifice, and growth. Though the silent battles may feel overwhelming, the rewards are immeasurable—the joy of raising a child, shaping a life, and discovering a love deeper than anything imagined.

Whether partnered or single, every parent's love **is enough**—and their efforts matter more than they know.

The Journey of a Single Father – Amir's Story

Amir, a 32-year-old banker from Tamil Nadu, never imagined he would have to raise his son, Kabir, alone. When his wife tragically passed away during the COVID-19 pandemic, his world turned upside down. Overnight, he went from being a loving husband and father to a grieving widower and a single parent.

With a demanding job and a three-year-old who needed him the most, Amir faced an uphill battle—emotionally, physically, and mentally.

Challenges Faced

- The sudden loss of his wife left Amir emotionally shattered. He had to navigate his own grief while being strong for Kabir.

- He had no one to share parenting decisions, daily struggles, or small moments of joy.

- Managing a full-time job while being present for his son felt like an impossible balancing act. He constantly battled guilt—feeling like he wasn't giving his best to either work or parenting.

- Society's stereotypes about single fathers made things harder. Many doubted his ability to handle the emotional and nurturing aspects of raising a child alone.

- He had to learn everyday tasks like preparing meals, managing bedtime routines, and comforting Kabir when he asked for his mother.

- Seeking help felt difficult—he feared it would make him seem incapable.

Steps Amir Took to Overcome the Challenges

Keeping His Wife's Memory Alive

- Amir openly talked to Kabir about his mother, making sure she remained a part of their lives.

Creating a Safe Emotional Space

- He built a strong emotional bond with his son, encouraging him to express his feelings rather than suppress them.

Seeking Support

- He joined a single-parent support group, connecting with other fathers facing similar struggles.

Adjusting Work-Life Balance

- Amir requested flexible work hours, ensuring he could be available whenever Kabir needed him.

Strengthening the Father-Son Bond

- He made time for special moments—visiting parks, watching movies, and cooking meals together. Despite the absence of a mother figure, he filled their home with love, laughter, and stability.

Outcome

Through resilience and dedication, Amir embraced his role as a single father. Kabir grew up in a home filled with warmth, love, and emotional security.

Amir proved that single fathers are just as capable of providing emotional, mental, and physical care as single mothers. His journey stands as a testament to the strength of single dads everywhere—showing that, despite hardships, a father's love can build a strong, happy, and thriving child.

Chapter 8:
Holding On to Letting Go

Just when we think we've figured out parenting, our children move into a new phase—bringing fresh challenges, joys, and lessons. Parenting is a journey of constant change. From sleepless newborn nights to watching them step into adulthood, each stage is a bittersweet blend of love, worry, and pride.

The Transition Journey

The newborn phase is a mix of exhaustion and pure magic. The nights feel endless, filled with feedings, diaper changes, and the soft touch of tiny fingers wrapped around ours.

As parents, we give up sleep, time, and even parts of ourselves, but in return, we receive irreplaceable moments—

their first smile, their first steps, their first words. In those early days, our entire world revolved around them, and we wouldn't have it any other way.

Then comes the boundless energy of toddlerhood. The sleepless nights turn into action-packed days—chasing little feet, baby-proofing every inch of the house, and answering a million "Why?" questions.

This phase is filled with laughter, tantrums, and endless curiosity. They test our patience in ways we never imagined, yet their innocence and wonder make it all worthwhile.

As they grow, we begin to feel them pulling away, little by little. Suddenly, we are no longer the center of their universe. They make new friends, explore new interests, and form opinions of their own.

We watch as they stumble and rise, celebrating their victories and comforting them in their defeats. And while we still want to hold them close, we start realizing that part of our role is to let them go.

Then come the teenage years—a new kind of challenge, one that requires more patience and understanding than ever before. Their eyes roll, their words become fewer, and their world expands beyond what we can see.

They crave independence but still need our guidance, even if they won't admit it. This phase teaches us that parenting is about trust—trusting them to make their own choices, trusting ourselves to guide them wisely, and trusting that the foundation we've built will carry them forward.

And then, before we know it, they are stepping into full independence. Whether it's college, a career, or starting a family of their own, they begin to build a life separate from ours. This is the true test of parenthood—letting go, knowing we've done our job. It's never easy, but it is the greatest act of love. It means we have raised a strong, kind, and capable human being who is ready to face the world.

The Heart of Parenthood

Parenting is a journey of holding on and learning to let go. Each phase has its struggles, but also its own special joys. We may no longer rock them to sleep, chase them around the house, or be their first call when something exciting happens—but in our hearts, they will always be our little munchkins.

Because no matter how much they grow, our love for them remains the same—constant, unwavering, and forever.

It's in the way we still pause when we see their baby pictures, remembering their tiny hands wrapped around our fingers. It's in the way we smile when we hear their favorite childhood song or spot their old stuffed toy tucked away in a corner. It's in the way we still worry, even when they assure us they're fine.

Parenthood is knowing that our arms may not always hold them, but our hearts always will. It's realizing that even as they carve their paths, a part of us walks with them—through every challenge, every triumph, every moment.

We may no longer kiss their scraped knees, but we will always be their safe place. We may not have all the answers, but we will always be their guiding light.

Because love in parenthood is not measured by proximity, but by the unbreakable bond that time, distance, and change can never erase. No matter where life takes them, they will always carry a piece of our hearts with them.

And that is the true beauty of parenting—it never really ends; it just transforms.

Aditi's Story – A Parent's Journey Through Different Phases

Aditi, a 40-year-old working mother from Delhi, always believed that parenthood was a beautiful and fulfilling journey. But she never realized how challenging, ever-changing, and transformative it would be—shaping her in ways she never imagined.

Her daughter, Samayra, is now 18 and about to leave for college. As Aditi reflects on the journey from newborn to adulthood, she sees the highs, the struggles, and the invaluable lessons she learned along the way.

The Different Phases of Parenthood

The Newborn Phase – Love, Exhaustion & Firsts

When Samayra was born, Aditi was overwhelmed with love but also exhausted beyond measure. The sleepless nights felt endless—feeding, rocking, soothing, only to wake up again for the next feed.

As a first-time mother, she constantly questioned herself:

"Am I doing this right?"

"Is she eating enough?"

"Am I a good mother?"

Amid the exhaustion, one moment changed everything—Samayra's first smile. In that instant, all the sleepless nights and self-doubt faded. Aditi realized that love and patience would always guide her through the hardest moments.

The Toddler Phase – Chaos, Guilt & Unconditional Joy

As Samayra grew, sleepless nights turned into energy-filled days. She was everywhere—climbing, running, exploring. Aditi spent her days on high alert, making sure Samayra didn't put something dangerous in her mouth or run too fast on the playground.

Balancing her career and motherhood became overwhelming. She felt guilty leaving her at daycare but knew she was working hard to create a better future for her daughter.

Despite the exhaustion, moments like hearing Samayra say "Mama" for the first time and watching her take her first steps made every struggle worth it.

The School Phase – Letting Go, Little by Little

The first day of school was harder for Aditi than it was for Samayra. For the past few years, Samayra had been her whole world, and now she had to send her off to make new friends, learn new things, and slowly build a life beyond her mother's arms.

As the years passed, Samayra became more independent, choosing her clothes, packing her school bag, and making small decisions. Aditi watched with pride and a touch of sadness as her little girl started growing into her own person.

The Teenage Phase – Distance, Patience & Silent Love

- By the time Samayra turned 12, her world shifted. Friends became her priority, conversations with her mother grew shorter, and she often retreated to her room with headphones on.

- At first, Aditi felt hurt. *Was she losing her daughter?* But then she realized—this was just another phase, another challenge.

- She found small ways to reconnect—planning movie nights, chatting over coffee, listening without judgment, and simply being there when Samayra needed her.

- It took years of patience—years of giving space without letting go completely. But one evening, when Samayra came to her and shared something personal, without being asked, Aditi knew she had done something right. Their bond was still strong, just evolving.

The Letting Go Phase – Pride, Pain & A New Beginning

- Now, at 18, Samayra is preparing to leave for college abroad. Aditi watches her pack, her heart heavy yet proud. The little girl who once held her hand so tightly is now stepping into the world on her own.

- For years, she had prepared for this moment, yet she wasn't ready to accept it.
- Letting go is painful, but it is also a sign of success. Her daughter has grown into a strong, independent young woman, ready to chase her dreams. And that, Aditi realizes, is the true goal of parenthood.

The Essence of Parenthood

Parenthood is a journey of **constant evolution**. Just when we feel we have it figured out, everything changes again.

- *Letting go is just as important as holding on.* Every stage of parenting teaches us to loosen our grip a little more.
- *The love between a parent and child never fades.* Even as they grow, they carry a part of us with them wherever they go.

Parenting isn't about controlling every phase—it's about embracing each moment, guiding our children, and preparing them to stand on their own. And in the end, that's what makes the journey so incredibly beautiful.

Chapter 9: Children Teach Us

Children teach us to live life to the fullest, embracing both the ups and downs while finding joy in small achievements. Their ability to see everyone as special and unique reminds us of the importance of inclusivity and tolerance. They are the best models of forgiveness, showing us how to let go of grudges and move forward with ease.

In the rush of responsibilities and the pursuit of success, we often forget what truly matters. But through their laughter, curiosity, and pure hearts, children become our greatest teachers. They show us the value of human connections and the beauty of unconditional love.

Their endless "Why?" questions spark curiosity and encourage us to explore new ideas. One of the greatest lessons we can learn from them is to express our feelings—whether joy, sadness, or anger—without fear. They remind us to be authentic and honest, both with ourselves and with others.

A child sees and creates magic in everyday moments. They remind us that life is full of little wonders—if only we take the time to notice.

As adults, we become occupied with work, worries, and routines. But when we truly listen to their endless questions, engage in their imaginary worlds, and watch them explore, we rediscover the beauty in things we once took for granted.

The best thing about children is that they don't dwell on the past or stress about the future. They live in the **NOW**—fully immersed in their play, their laughter, and their emotions. As parents, we often find ourselves worrying about the future. But they remind us that these moments won't last forever. They teach us to slow down, cherish the present, and truly be with them, rather than just around them.

Parenting comes with self-doubt. *Am I doing enough? Am I doing it right?* But children don't seek perfect parents—they seek present parents. They won't remember the spotless house, the perfect meals, or the expensive gifts. They will remember the cuddles after a bad dream, the laughter during a silly game, and the times we paused everything just to listen to them.

They remind us that love is felt in the small, everyday moments—the gentle words, the patience when they struggle, and the way we show up for them, no matter what.

In teaching them, we are the ones who learn the most. Our children show us how to wonder, how to live in the moment, and how to love without conditions.

Perhaps the greatest lesson of all is this: While we shape them into who they will become, they remind us of who we once were—and who we can be again.

Navya's Story – The Lessons a Child Taught Me

Navya, a 30-year-old marketing professional and mother to a a 4-year-old boy, always believed in structure, perfection, and planning. She meticulously balanced work and parenting, ensuring that everything in her household ran smoothly.

However, in her pursuit of being the *perfect mother*, she often found herself exhausted, overwhelmed, and disconnected from the simple joys of motherhood.

The Challenges She Faced

The Pressure of Perfection – Navya felt she had to do everything right. From preparing nutritious meals to engaging her son in meaningful activities and keeping the house spotless, any deviation made her feel like she was failing as a parent.

Always Rushing – Her life revolved around to-do lists, deadlines, and responsibilities. Bedtime stories were cut short, playtime was interrupted by emails, and she was constantly in a hurry.

Physically Present, But Emotionally Distant – Her son would excitedly show her his drawings or ask her to play, but she was often too preoccupied. She realized she was *there* but not *really there*.

The Moment of Realization

One evening, after a long day at work, Navya was rushing through her son's bedtime routine when he looked up at her and asked,

"Mama, why are you always in a hurry? Can we just cuddle for a little while?"

His words hit her hard. In that moment, she realized that while she was striving to be a *perfect* parent, all her child truly wanted was **her presence, her love, and her time**.

The Lessons She Learned

Slowing Down – Navya started listening to her son's endless stories—how the moon made him smile, how he wanted to shine like a star, or how he loved making shadow animals on the wall.

Embracing the Mess – She let go of rigid routines and began enjoying **spontaneous dance parties, messy art sessions, and bedtime giggles.** She realized that *the best parenting moments are often unplanned.*

Prioritizing Connection Over Perfection – She understood that skipping a home-cooked meal for a fries party wouldn't harm her son. In fact, these small, carefree moments helped them bond even more.

The Beautiful Outcome

As Navya embraced this new perspective, her bond with her son grew stronger. She **rediscovered the joy of motherhood**—not in perfection, but in presence.

She realized that children don't need a perfect home, perfect meals, or perfect schedules.

They just need **love, patience, and a parent who is truly there**.

In the end, it's not about doing everything right—it's about being present for the little heart that loves us the most

Chapter 10:
Finding Myself in the Moonlight

Motherhood was supposed to be a time of joy, but for me, it became a test of endurance. As I carried my daughter inside me, I also carried the weight of loneliness, betrayal, and pain. And in the silence of my home, where love should have been, I found myself alone—both physically and emotionally.

The echoes of my past haunted me. The pain of my abortion, the judgment that followed, and the forced isolation during my pregnancy broke me in ways I never imagined. I longed for my father's presence, his comforting words, his unwavering belief in me. But he was gone, and I had to face this storm without him.

Yet, in the darkest nights, the moonlight found me. And with it, I found a new purpose—**my daughter**.

She became the light I never knew I needed, the reason I chose to rise instead of crumble. Every time she smiled, I felt my father's love through her. Every time she held my finger, I was reminded that I was not alone.

I now realize that **strength is not about who stands beside you but about who rises despite being alone.** My father taught me resilience, kindness, and self-respect, and I will pass these lessons on to my daughter.

· *She will know that her worth is not defined by others' acceptance but by her own self-love.*

· *She will know that silence in the face of injustice is never an option.*

· She will know that she is never truly alone—because I will always be there for her, just as my father's love remains with me.

As I look at the moon tonight, I no longer feel lost. Instead, I see a reflection of my journey—a journey from **pain to purpose, from loneliness to love, from a broken woman to a strong mother.**

The moon no longer reminds me of what I have lost. **It reminds me of what I have found—myself.**

And in that moonlight, I know I am exactly where I am meant to be.

In the hush of night, where moonlight glows,
I stood alone with tales only silence knows.
A heart once fractured, a soul weighed down,
Yet in the dark, I refused to drown.
They turned away, their warmth grew cold,
The walls around me, distant and bold.
Unspoken words, but scars ran deep,
I swallowed tears, dreams left to keep.
I longed for my father, his steady hand,
His voice, his wisdom to help me stand.
Though time had taken him far from sight,
His love remained—my guiding light.
Then she arrived—my dawn, my grace,
My reason to rise, my safe embrace.
Her tiny fingers curled in mine,
A love so fierce, a bond divine.
No longer lost, no longer weak,

Her laughter gave my soul its speak.
I'll teach her strength, I'll teach her grace,
To walk with fire, to claim her space.
She'll know her worth, she'll stand up tall,
Unshaken, fearless—she won't fall.
For through my trials, I came to see,
The strongest love was born in me.
The moon still shines, and now I know—
It never left, it helped me grow.
And in its glow, so pure, so bright,
I found myself, bathed in its light.

www.ingramcontent.com/pod-product-compliance
Lightning Source LLC
LaVergne TN
LVHW041545070526
838199LV00046B/1841